TEACHING TO
TRANSFORM
NOT INFORM

VOLUME 1

Resources by Dr. W. Bradley Simon

1. TEACHING TO TRANSFORM NOT INFORM 1: Foundational Principles for Making an Informational Sunday School Lesson…TRANSFORMATIONAL

2. DVD Video Companion for TEACHING TO TRANSFORM NOT INFORM 1: Foundational Principles for Making an Informational Sunday School Lesson…TRANSFORMATIONAL

3. TEACHING TO TRANSFORM NOT INFORM 2: How to Teach a Transformational Sunday School Lesson…STEP-BY-STEP

4. DVD Video Companion for TEACHING TO TRANSFORM NOT INFORM 2: How to Teach a Transformational Sunday School Lesson…STEP-BY-STEP

When purchasing books for a group, see the www.M2820.com store for bulk pricing.

Additional Resources

If you are training your teachers to craft and teach, high-impact, life-altering lessons, visit our website for additional resources (www.M2820.com).

TEACHING TO
TRANSFORM
NOT INFORM

VOLUME 1

Foundational Principles for Making
an Informational Sunday School Lesson...
TRANSFORMATIONAL

W. BRADLEY SIMON, PH.D.

28:20
TEACHING TO TRANSFORM
www.M2820.com

For additional companion teaching resources for this book or copyright inquires:

M28:20 Bluffton, SC 29910
www.M2820.com, info@M2820.com

Printed in the United States of America

All Scripture quotations, unless otherwise noted, are taken from The Holy Bible, New International Version®. NIV®. Copyright © 1973, 1978, 1984, 2011 by Biblica, Inc.™ Used by permission. All rights reserved worldwide. www.zondervan.com

Scripture quotations marked NASB are taken from the NEW AMERICAN STAN-DARD BIBLE®, Copyright © 1960, 1962, 1963, 1968, 1971, 1972, 1973, 1975, 1977, 1995 by The Lockman Foundation. Used by permission. www.Lockman.org

Scripture quotations in italics or bold have been added by the author for emphasis.

Simon, W. Bradley, 1962–
Teaching to TRANSFORM Not Inform 1: Foundational Principles for Making an Informational Sunday School Lesson...TRANSFORMATIONAL (Sunday School Teacher Training)
  ISBN 978-1-939257-11-6 (paperback)
  Subject Headings: Christian education—Teacher training. 2. Sunday schools — Teaching methods. 3. Sunday schools — Teacher training.

Cover design by Bill Foster and Dr. W. Bradley Simon
Interior design by Dr. W. Bradley Simon

To Kelly,
my godly wife,
who has loved, encouraged, and supported me
for more than half my life.

Then Jesus came to them and said, "All authority in heaven and on earth has been given to me. Therefore go and make disciples of all nations, baptizing them in the name of the Father and of the Son and of the Holy Spirit, and teaching them to obey everything I have commanded you. And surely I am with you always, to the very end of the age."

— Matthew 28:18-20

Table of Contents

Chapter Outlines

Ch: 3–How You Teach MORE by Teaching LESS
(Part 1)

See more life change by covering fewer
verses/topics at a greater depth

CH: 4–How You Teach MORE by Teaching LESS
(PART 2)

Choose the most effective format.
Which one do you use?

CH: 5–Become One of the Imperfect People God Uses

How to boldly teach and challenge your class
despite your past and weaknesses

CH: 6–Create a Ripple That Continues into Eternity

Your impact does not stop at the end of class ... it ripples from person to person to person all the way into eternity

Introduction

In Matthew 28:19–20, Jesus gives teachers a clear and concise teaching goal: *"Therefore go and make disciples… teaching them to obey everything I have commanded you."* He does not say to teach people *what* to obey or even *how* to obey; rather, Jesus says, *"make disciples… teaching them **to obey**."* As a result, Jesus makes life-altering transformation (not simply information or explanation) our primary teaching goal.

Consequently, the *Teaching to TRANSFORM Not Inform* series focuses on showing you how to turn informationally or educationally oriented Bible lessons into life-altering transformational ones. You will learn how to teach not only the head but also the heart, which results in changed lives. You will learn how to integrate transformational principles throughout your teaching, so you can fulfill the Great Commission as a Bible teacher.

This first book lays the biblical foundation for teaching the attitudes, priorities, and goals that help you maximize your impact as a teacher. As you work through additional books and seminars within this series, they build upon previous ones giving you a linear path for developing more and more advanced teaching skills. For example, the next book in the series, *Teaching to TRANSFORM Not Inform 2: How to Teach a Transformational Sunday School Lesson…*

STEP-BY-STEP, builds upon the foundation presented in this book by giving you a simple, practical, step-by-step process for how to develop and teach a Bible lesson that changes hearts and transforms lives. It outlines the seven teaching elements that need to be in every lesson that has transformation as its main objective.

1

It's about Transformation, Not Simply Information and Explanation

Jesus calls you to fulfill the Great Commission by teaching them to obey

*Therefore go and make
disciples … teaching them to obey
everything I have commanded you.*

— Matthew 28:19–20

Chapter Outline / Notes

I. **What is the goal of M28:20 teaching?**

A. For "Teaching Tom," it's all about explanation

- what is done w/ the teaching
  is their responsibility
- focused on what was said / how it was
  said

B. For Jesus, it's all about transformation

II. **Transformation is the goal of M28:20 teaching**

A. "Go and make disciples" (Matthew 28:19)

"make"

1. Jesus doesn't say, *"Force people to become disciples"*

- guilt/manipulation

2. Jesus doesn't say, *"Teach people **how** to become disciples"*

3. Jesus says, *"Go and make disciples"*

B. "Teaching them to obey"

*1. Jesus doesn't say, "**Force** them to obey"*

*2. Jesus doesn't say, "Teach them **what** I have commanded"*

*3. Jesus doesn't say, "Teach them **how** to obey"*

*4. Jesus says, "Teach them **to obey**"*

" Teaching how" vs "Teaching To"

*A*S A TEACHER, YOU NEVER REALLY KNOW how much of an impact you are having on others until they become a little vulnerable and tell you something like this: "You know, I was going to get a divorce, but what you said made a lot of sense, and I've decided to work through it." Individuals rarely admit such near misses, but when they do, it gives you a glimpse of how your teaching is changing their lives.

We all know people change because God is at work in them. We realize the truths we share are not our own, but God's. Nevertheless, God has chosen to work through us as we teach his Word, but what happens when it doesn't feel like our teaching is making a difference in people's lives?

I remember one teacher had spent several months teaching through a particular study. Then, a few months after the series concluded, several who had attended the Bible study chose to do the exact opposite of what the teacher had just spent several months teaching.

You talk about discouraging; that was really discouraging for him. Upon reflection, he said,

> I feel like they understood what I said, and I tried to be as clear, thorough, biblically oriented, and practical as possible. Why, then, did they choose to do the opposite? I guess the saying is true: you can lead a horse to the water, but you can't make it drink. Or, from a teacher's perspective, you can tell listeners what the Bible says, but you can't make them obey.

I. What is the goal of M28:20 teaching?

After a few experiences like this, it is easy to develop a teaching philosophy that says, "My goal as a teacher is to explain the text and show how we can apply it to our lives. However, it is my listeners' responsibility to listen, ask any clarifying questions, and obey."

A. For "Teaching Tom," it's all about explanation

Actually, I had a teacher tell me something similar to this. I'll refer to him as "Teaching Tom." Teaching Tom said to me, "My responsibility as a teacher is to explain the text and show how we can apply it to our lives; however, what my listeners do with that information is their responsibility." He concluded his responsibility began and ended with the lesson. What took place outside of that hour had little impact or bearing on his own teaching style or methodology. In short, his goal focuses on information, explanation, and presentation.

B. For Jesus, it's all about transformation

Teaching Tom's philosophy may initially sound right, but is it biblically accurate, especially in light of verses such as Matthew 28:18–20?

> Then Jesus came to them and said, "All authority in heaven and on earth has been given to me. 19 Therefore go and make disciples of all nations, baptizing them in the name of the Father and of the Son and of the Holy Spirit, 20 and teaching

them to obey everything I have commanded you.
And surely I am with you always, to the very end
of the age."

Let's look a little closer at these verses and answer a
few related questions.

1. To whom is Matthew 28:18–20 directed?
   A. Jesus' disciples.
   B. Jesus' disciples, plus people such as pastors and
      missionaries.
   C. All believers, including you and me.

2. Circle the words in Matthew 28:18–20 that indicate
   what Jesus is instructing us to do.

3. In verse 20, underline all the words that refer to our
   goal in teaching.

4. What is the goal of Teaching Tom's philosophy? Which
   parts are correct and which parts may be biblically inac-
   curate? Does it accurately reflect the goal of teaching
   as given in Matthew 28:18–20?

   Again, Teaching Tom said, "My goal as a teacher is
   to explain the text and show how we can apply it to
   our lives. However, it is my listeners' responsibility
   to listen, ask any clarifying questions, and obey."

5. How should we respond if our teaching does not change lives?

Let's next answer the above questions by taking a closer look at Matthew 28:19–20.

II. Transformation is the goal of M28:20 teaching
A. "Go and make disciples" (Matthew 28:19)

Let's think through a few different responses we may have when our teaching doesn't seem to bring change in listeners' lives. Obviously, God doesn't call us to force listeners to obey. It is clear that listeners are responsible for their actions, and they must choose to obey. However, God has called us to focus on more than information, explanation, and presentation.

Let's begin by looking at Matthew 28:19:

Therefore go and make disciples of all nations, baptizing them in the name of the Father and of the Son and of the Holy Spirit.

*1. Jesus doesn't say, "**Force** people to become disciples"*
Notice the first few words in verse 19: "Go and make disciples." Jesus is clearly *not* telling us to "Go and *force* people to become disciples;" however, when speakers use guilt and manipulation to bring about change, it appears they are trying to force people to become disciples. Even though this form of teaching may bring about

some type of change in listeners, it is an unhealthy, short-term change that fails to produce the lifestyle God desires.

2. Jesus doesn't say, "Teach people *how* to become disciples"

Similarly, Matthew 28:19 does not say, "Go and teach people *how* to become disciples." Even though this is included in what Jesus says, it still lacks all he says. If you think about it, this was Teaching Tom's position. He told the class how to become a disciple, but what they did with that information was up to them. His focus was on the classroom time. It was on what he said and how he said it. His responsibility began when listeners arrived and ended when they left. If his teaching didn't change lives, hey, that wasn't his responsibility. Teaching Tom's goal was teaching what the Bible said and how one can apply it.

3. Jesus says, "Go and *make* disciples"

What, then, is Jesus calling us to do? It's only four words, so let's look at it again. Jesus says, "go and *make* disciples" (Matthew 28:19).

This is a fair and balanced command. Jesus isn't telling us to *force* people to become disciples or simply to give information on *how* to become a disciple; rather, his focus and command is in the center: "Go and *make* disciples."

- You're not forcing people,

    but you're also not just giving information.
- You're not demanding, intimidating, or manipulating,

but you're also not just suggesting.
- Your focus is on the classroom,
        but it also extends beyond the classroom.
- Your focus is on what you say,
        but it is also on how it impacts and changes people's lives.
- It is a call to "make disciples."

B. "Teaching them to obey"

Let's next look at Matthew 28:20 where Jesus continues to define our teaching goal.

> Therefore go and make disciples of all nations, baptizing them in the name of the Father and of the Son and of the Holy Spirit, and *teaching them to obey everything I have commanded you.* And surely I am with you always, to the very end of the age.

1. Jesus doesn't say, "**Force** them to obey"

As in verse 19, Jesus does not tell us to "*force* people to obey" by using guilt, peer pressure, or some other form of manipulation; rather, he says, "*teach* them to obey everything I have commanded you."

2. Jesus doesn't say, "Teach them **what** I have commanded"

Similarly, the command is not simply to "Teach them *what* I have commanded you." When teachers assume this is their goal, their teaching often sounds something like this:

"In our passage today, Paul was telling the Corinthians to do this and that in order to bring unity in the church. The reason Paul had to say this was because the Corinthians were involved in a first-century practice where ..." and the teacher would supply the relevant background information. Then, the teacher continues, "In this next verse, Paul said this because of that and the Greek word he used here was ..." and again, some more information. By the end of the lesson, listeners may have a lot of information and explanation, but often lack transformation.

It actually makes a lot of sense why so many Bible study teachers follow this format. After all, this is the teaching goal and methodology the public school system has modeled for us throughout most of our school years. By default, we learn that teachers provide information, such as dates, facts, theories, principles, and more. Consequently, unless someone has taught us otherwise, when we become a Bible study teacher, we likewise provide information pertaining to biblical events, dates, background material, Old Testament history, New Testament customs, theology, and more. All good stuff, but Jesus calls us not to give information, but to make disciples.

3. Jesus doesn't say, "Teach them **how** to obey"

Last, in Matthew 28:20, Jesus does not say, "Teach them *how* to obey." Like Teaching Tom, teachers within this category agree that we should teach what the Bible says as well as *how* to apply it. Of course, they are correct and application should be a part of every lesson, but it still falls short of what Jesus calls us to do. There is still a difference between "teaching them *how* to obey" and "teaching them *to* obey."

When our goal is to teach people either "*what* the Bible says" or "*how* they can obey," our focus tends to be on the presentation as opposed to whether or not anyone's life changed. After the lesson, we ask presentation-oriented questions, such as "Was I clear? Was the lesson interesting? Did you understand what I was saying?" Of course, a clear, interesting, understandable lesson is important and necessary, but, as we all know, a clear, interesting, understandable lesson does not always lead to "teaching them to obey."

*4. Jesus says, "Teach them **to obey**"*

Clearly, our goal needs to be on "teaching them *to obey*." When this is our focus, our teaching shifts from information to transformation. All teachers agree we should clearly teach biblical truths and principles, but the most effective teachers are always aiming for transformation. Their goal is interpretation, contemplation, explanation, application, and finally, transformation. Matthew 28:20 calls us to be Transformational Teachers, not simply Informational Teachers. It is a calling to transform the heart, not simply inform the mind.

*Information and Explanation
are foundational to our teaching, but
transformation is the goal.*

Understanding this distinction and personally accepting the balanced responsibility is the first step in becoming an M28:20 Transformational Teacher, because it drives us to ask ourselves growth-oriented questions:

- What is the difference between a teacher who teaches people *what* or *how* to obey and a teacher who teaches them *to* obey?
- Even though most teachers teach *what* the Bible says and *how* we can apply it, are transformational teachers doing more?
- What kind of impact do these small variations have on listeners?

The answers to these questions are what this series is all about. In the next chapter, we're going to look at one of the biggest obstacles to transformational teaching: the Scratchpad. If you are unaware of how it works, then your teaching will make it from the Bible to the listener's Scratchpad, but it may get stuck right there, never making it into their heart. Listeners may learn *what* Jesus commanded and *how* they can obey, but they may never actually obey. They believe your lesson is applicable for others, but for one reason or another, it won't work in their own life. Your listeners want to live a godly life, and by taking just a couple of minutes in your teaching time, you can help them do so by helping them transfer the truth from their Scratchpad to their heart.

Leading a teacher training seminar?

If you believe the teachers within your church would benefit from the *Teaching to TRANSFORM Not Inform* series, consider leading them in a study using the companion DVD for this book that leads your teachers through this material. Also, see the store at M2820.com for bulk book pricing.

Another possibility includes hosting a live *Teaching to TRANSFORM Not Inform* conference at your church. Our goal is to train teachers to fulfill the Great Commission through their teaching ministry at no cost to your church or organization. This is possible when a few different churches participate in the training. To see how this works, see the "Conferences" page on our website.

2

How to Transform Both the Head and Heart

Build a bridge from the Bible to the head,
around roadblocks, then to their heart

*Apply your heart to instruction and
your ears to words of knowledge.*

— Proverbs 23:12

Chapter Outline / Notes

I. **Initially, I learned how to build a bridge from the Bible to the head (Scratchpad)**

   A. Delivery style

   different things he pointed out

   B. Lesson structure

   C. Relational aspects

II. **But I discovered I still didn't always know how to help listeners…**

   A. …integrate difficult truths into their lives

   B. …transfer difficult truths from their Scratchpad to their heart

C. ... discover and remove roadblocks

III. Later, I learned how to build a bridge from the head to the heart

A. Do roadblocks matter?

B. Roadblocks must be addressed

C. Address roadblocks at the beginning of the lesson

✱ Balance between Spirit applying
it and laziness in responsibility
✱ Can't take all responsibility
in our teaching for
disobedience

IN THE LAST CHAPTER, WE SAW HOW easy it is to incorporate into our teaching the wonderfully modeled teaching goals and methodology used within the public school system. Incorporating these teaching principles into your own teaching will certainly help you develop into a highly effective communicator who is able to clearly explain the text. However, one nagging question remains: Even though these principles and techniques will help you become a better informational teacher, are they all that is needed to develop into a highly effective transformational teacher?

I became a Christian in 1980, and within a few months, God began to grow within me a love for teaching and a calling to this type of ministry. I began to consume books, seminars, and classes related to teaching and preaching methodology. Most of the resources I came across related to informational teaching principles, so that is what I ended up learning first.

I. Initially, I learned how to build a bridge from the Bible to the head (Scratchpad)

A. Delivery style

Some of these resources focused on the importance of delivery style. Below is a summary of some of the key principles you should incorporate into your teaching:

- Stand up straight.
- Don't put your hands in your pockets.
- Don't fiddle with your ring.

- Don't lean on the podium.
- Remember to smile and make it fun.
- Make eye contact for two to four seconds.
- Vary the tone and volume of your voice.
- Vary the rate at which you speak. Most Westerners speak around 130 to 150 words per minute during a regular conversation. Speaking slower than this may result in listeners getting bored and thinking about other things; speaking faster can add interest. Listeners view fast speakers (up to 195 words per minute) as more credible, intelligent, knowledgeable, and persuasive than slow speakers (around 100 words per minute). Note: audio books are voiced around 150–160 words per minute, auctioneers speak around 250–400 wpm, and the average reading rate is around 200–300 wpm.
- Vary your energy: too little energy is boring; too much energy is stressful.
- Include one- to three-second pauses to emphasize key points.
- Move around the room as you talk.
- Gesture while you speak using animated hand and arm movements along with facial expressions.
- Ask a question, then pause for at least three to five seconds so listeners can develop an answer.
- Ensure discussions stay focused on the topic.
- Use visual aids.
- Practice, practice, practice, but don't sound canned.

All great stuff.

B. Lesson structure

Other times, the resources focused on the lesson's structure or organization:

- Tell 'em what you're going to tell 'em. Tell 'em. Then, tell 'em what you told 'em.
- Make sure the introduction grabs their attention by including a joke, personal story, or other attention-getting element.
- And always end with a strong pre-planned conclusion.

C. Relational aspects

Still, other resources focused on the importance of deepening your relationship with your listeners by spending time with them outside of the classroom. In addition to the mutual edification and encouragement that comes from these deepened relationships, they will also help you better orient your material to everyone's specific phase of life.

II. But I discovered I still didn't always know how to help listeners ...

A. ... integrate difficult truths into their lives

All this information was essential for developing as a teacher, but something still seemed to be missing. The resources taught me how to structure and deliver a lesson, but that didn't always seem to be enough. Even though they explained how to teach a relevant, applicable Bible lesson, they were a little less clear on what to do if some of the listeners had a hard time personally accepting and applying the truth.

Consequently, I had a pretty good understanding of how to transfer truths from the Bible to the cognitive part of the mind where listeners understood the principles and application. However, I didn't always know how to help those who understood the lesson but failed to integrate it into their life for one reason or another.

I knew how to explain *what* the Bible said and *how* listeners could apply it, but that didn't always result in a *changed* life. At that point, it would be easy to assume Teaching Tom's solution to the problem and conclude, "God calls teachers to teach his Word, so if some don't apply it to their lives, I can't do anything about that." However, I knew that solution wasn't right, so I began asking questions: "What are my lessons missing? What would help listeners not only cognitively understand the information but apply it as well? How can I modify my lessons so they are more transformational?"

B. ... transfer difficult truths from their Scratchpad to their heart

To answer these questions, I began to read and study anything and everything that might provide a solution. I was looking for a teaching methodology that helped listeners, first, understand the lesson, and second, overcome any barriers that hindered them from applying it to their life.

I was trying to figure out how to build a bridge from what listeners cognitively understood on the one side, to their personal set of beliefs, views, actions, values, attitudes, priorities, hopes, dreams, opinions, prejudices, will, and commitments that were on the other side. What I discovered was that, after they cognitively understood *what* the Bible said and *how* they could apply it to their life, sometimes the truth stayed right there, in that cognitive area of their head where they simply understood the truth.

Helping them integrate the truths into their lives was challenging. Even though they heard and comprehended the lesson, that didn't always mean they personally accepted its truths and application as their own. At times, it seemed as if some sort of roadblock kept what they understood in their head from being accepted into their heart. Even though they understood the truths, concepts, and application, that didn't mean they automatically believed it, accepted it, valued it, committed to it, and made it a priority in their life.

Even though listeners may comprehend
your lesson, roadblocks hinder them
from personally accepting it.

It's almost as if listeners have a public Scratchpad in their head that is entirely different from their closely guarded private list of beliefs, opinions, values, and attitudes they hold in their heart. Their Scratchpad acts like public storage for various ideas and thoughts. Throughout each and every day, including Sunday when you teach, it's as if your listeners freely write down on their Scratchpad all the views, ideas, and values they hear. Sometimes they accept particular truths and integrate them into their life. Other times, the truths make it to their Scratchpad, hit a roadblock, and stop right there, never making it to their heart, where life change becomes a reality.

C. ... discover and remove roadblocks

For example, let's say you teach a series on prayer. By the end of the series, everyone understands *what* the Bible says about prayer and *how* they can apply the teaching. For some, they already want to grow in their prayer lives, so they gladly accept and integrate the principles into their lives. For others, however, their prayer life doesn't change. Why? Well, maybe it's because your teaching clearly made it from the Bible to their Scratchpad but stopped right there because it hit a roadblock. They understood the *what* and *how*, but some personal challenge, experience, misunderstanding, doubt, justification, rationalization, or objection caused them to resist the teaching and keep it on their Scratchpad.

It may be that some of them believe God answers prayer, just not their prayers. Sure, universally speaking, God answers prayer ... after all, it's in the Bible ... right? But personally speaking, they don't believe God will answer their prayers because they have prayed many times and nothing changed. So, yes, generally speaking, they understand and believe God answers prayer, but since it doesn't seem as though he answers their personal prayers, they seldom pray.

*Listeners believe
some principles are universally true,
but not personally applicable.*

Even though they understand *what* the biblical text says about prayer and *how* they can apply it, it's unlikely they will do so until this roadblock is removed. Even if you taught a fifty-part series on prayer, if this roadblock remains, little will change.

Or, maybe you have a woman in your class whose mother became ill when she was young. Even though she prayed and prayed and prayed, her mom still died a long, drawn-out death. For this woman, the whole topic of prayer is painful. She may pleasantly sit and listen to your lesson, and if you are clear, she will fully understand what you are saying, but she is not going to start praying again until she is able to deal with this painful experience. For her, the biblical truths will stay right there on her cognitive Scratchpad until someone gently helps her remove the roadblock that keeps the painful information from entering her closely protected and sensitive heart.

III. Later, I learned how to build a bridge from the head to the heart

A. Do roadblocks matter?

Again, the question arises, "Do I need to be concerned with helping listeners remove these roadblocks?" And, the answer is this:

If your goal is to be an informational teacher and you are content with simply placing information on the listener's Scratchpad, then, no, you don't need to worry about these roadblocks since you can successfully place information on one's Scratchpad even with the barriers intact. However, if becoming an M28:20 Transformational Teacher is your goal, then, yes, these roadblocks are a major concern since they hinder people from embracing the biblical truths and integrating them into their lives.

B. Roadblocks must be addressed

Sometimes, teachers believe it is safer not to raise and discuss potential objections, problems, difficult questions, apparent contradictions, or other roadblocks related to the passage or lesson. After all, maybe no one else notices how one passage seems to contradict another or how the principle doesn't always appear to work in real life. Plus, highlighting them may upset the stability of some listeners' faith or beliefs.

On the one hand, these teachers are correct in that you should be conscious of your audience and not raise questions they are not asking or raise issues that are beyond their spiritual maturity level; but, on the other hand, you don't want to pretend that the pink elephant sitting on the back row is not there.

Unless you are teaching new believers, my guess is those in your class are sharp, and they are very aware of the pink elephant no matter how hard he tries to hide. Therefore, no matter how well you present your lesson, if you don't address the pink glow coming from the back row, your lesson will make it from the Bible to your listeners' Scratchpad, but fail to make it to their heart. That big pink elephant can't help but block the path that leads from the head to the heart.

Unaddressed pink elephants
can't help but block the path that
leads from the head to the heart.

C. Address roadblocks at the beginning of the lesson

So, when should you introduce potential problems listeners may have with what you are about to say? I believe it is often best to introduce them somewhere near the beginning of the lesson. You may not give a full explanation right then, but you can at least let everyone know that you will address the issues later in the lesson.

When you do this, you captivate your listeners because they realize that the lesson is about to depart from the typical humdrum type of lesson they have heard for the last 20 years. Everyone perks up and pays attention waiting to hear how you will answer a question they have never been able to answer.

On the other hand, if you begin your lesson without addressing common objections, listeners may tune you out even before you finish the introduction. They assume they know what you are about to say, and since this has never worked in their life before, they check out and begin thinking about something else.

So surprise them. At the very beginning, promise to address potential issues they have always wondered about. See if you can get them to physically sit up in their chair and lean forward in anticipation of what you are about to say.

Consider the following example of an introduction that promises to give solutions to common objections.

Do you ever find yourself saying, "If it's not one thing, it's another?" I know I do. It just seems like no matter what I'm trying to accomplish, some problem is always there to slow me down. Even if I solve that problem quicker than expected, two more pop up right after it. Moving forward is difficult because the road I'm on contains an infinite number of sharp corners, cutbacks, detours, and traffic jams. I drive and drive and drive, but seldom in the direction I want to go.

In our lesson today, we are going to look at a passage where God promises to make our paths straight. Let's look at it.

> Trust in the LORD with all your heart and lean not on your own understanding; in all your ways acknowledge him, and *he will make your paths straight.*
>
> — Proverbs 3:5–6

So, who would like God to "make your paths straight"? I know I would, so I'm all ears. Who would like to discover how they can finally move forward in life without all the problems and issues? Again, count me in [I raise my hand for all to see].

So, let's read the verse again to see what is needed on our part:

> *Trust* in the LORD with *all* your heart and *lean not* on your own understanding; in *all* your ways *acknowledge him*, and he will make your paths straight.

At this point, many teachers would be done with the introduction and begin the Bible study portion of the lesson. After all, they have shared the lesson's topic and primary verses. However, they failed to address the very questions these passages raise in their listeners' mind. Instead of drawing the class further into the study by promising to answer the questions everyone is wondering about, they give information that answers questions no one is asking. Look at how the last portion of the introduction deals with pertinent questions and creates a desire to hear the remainder of the lesson.

OK, so the principles within these verses seem simple enough, but they still leave me with a few questions. For example, if I'm trusting God, why do my paths seem to be anything but straight? I know I am trusting him, so could the problem be that I'm just not trusting him enough? Could it be that I'm trusting him, but just not with *all* my heart?

I don't know about you, but sometimes I wonder if I can actually consistently trust him with every single area of my life. You know what I mean? [And, of course, they do, so they are right there with you.] What happens, then, if one small part of me isn't trusting him in one particular area? Does that negate the entire promise? Is that why all these problems crop up in my life?

Also, when the verse says, "and lean not on your own understanding," what does that mean? Would it be wrong for me to follow logic if I also have a "feeling" inside telling me to do something different? How do I know when that feeling is God trying to redirect my steps? If I tend to follow my logic, is that the same thing as leaning on my own understanding? Maybe that's the source of all my problems.

Or, what if I had a financial crisis, and the only way to prevent defaulting on my house loan was to stop tithing for six months. Even though logic tells me to temporarily stop tithing, should I tithe anyway and "trust in the Lord" to provide the money some other way?

We all want God to "make our paths straight," so let's look at what it means to trust him, not lean on our own understanding, and acknowledge him in all our ways.

As you can see, I didn't answer all the questions up front, but I assured everyone I would explain them at some point within the lesson. I also asked some real-life questions that need to be answered before my listeners will be able to apply the Scripture to their lives, that is, before my listeners will be able to move the principle from their Scratchpad to their heart. Raising these questions early on helps listeners realize the lesson's value and how it will help them improve areas that they already realize need help.

As we proceed through the following chapters, we will discuss teaching techniques that help listeners integrate challenging truths into their lives. We will also discuss how you can help listeners dismantle roadblocks so your teaching impacts areas of their lives that may have been dormant for years. As your listeners grow and develop into fully committed Christ followers, you will fulfill the Great Commission by making disciples who obey all that Christ commanded.

Sticky Proverb

3

How You Teach MORE by Teaching LESS (PART 1)

See more life change by covering fewer verses/topics at a greater depth

*Instruct a wise man
and he will be wiser still;
teach a righteous man
and he will add to his learning.*

— Proverbs 9:9

Chapter Outline / Notes

I. The transformational riddle

II. The riddle's solution

    A. Determine your teaching goal

        1. Is your goal information or transformation?

        2. Is your goal an InfoTransformational lesson?

    B. For informational lessons, you "Teach More by Teaching More"

    C. For transformational lessons, you "Teach MORE by Teaching LESS"

        1."Teach LESS" in the sense of reducing the breadth of topics or verses covered

2. *"Teach LESS" by identifying the lesson's exact goal*

3. *"Teaching LESS" doesn't mean lessons are shorter; they are just more focused*

D. Center the lesson around the Sticky Proverb

1. *Listeners forget what they hear*

2. *Teachers forget what they studied*

3. *Listeners can take notes, but they must be reviewed*

4. *Centering your lesson around the Sticky Proverb helps everyone*

III. Sunday school curriculum

I **HAVE ALWAYS ENJOYED RIDDLES THAT REVEAL** how something that sounds impossible is possible or how something that appears to be completely wrong is, in fact, right. I still remember some of the riddles I heard as a child such as this one: "What grows bigger the more you take away from it?" Initially, I thought, "Well, nothing. I mean, how can something get bigger the more you take away from it?" Of course, when I heard the answer was a hole, I laughed because the impossible became possible in a single word.

I. The transformational riddle

In today's lesson, we are going to look at a riddle that also looks unsolvable; and yet when solved, it reveals one of the foundational principles for developing transformational lessons. Here it is:

How do you teach MORE by teaching LESS?

Like all riddles, initially it appears that any answer would be wrong, backward, or impossible; however, once you understand the answer, you understand how, in fact, you teach MORE by teaching LESS. The answer isn't a one-liner as with most riddles; rather, it will take most of the chapter to explain. By the end of the chapter, you will know how to teach more by excluding much of what you planned on including and by omitting many of the main points, sub-points, and illustrations you planned on presenting. It sounds wrong, right? It is a riddle that has taken years to solve, yet it is one worth solving, so let's get started.

II. The riddle's solution
A. Determine your teaching goal
1. Is your goal information or transformation?
Before preparing your lesson outline, establish the goal of the lesson: information or transformation. Of course, these goals are not mutually exclusive in that informational lessons transform lives and transformational lessons contain information. Nevertheless, each goal requires its own specific set of teaching principles.

When teaching an informational lesson, my primary goal is to transfer as much information as possible from my brain to your brain. Of course, I hope it impacts your life as well, but with an informational lesson, if I have to choose between information and application, information wins. Why? Because that is my goal: a cognitive information transfer.

For example, a lesson on the five points of Calvinism, a historical overview of the Old Testament, or the historical background of the book of Romans would probably be informational lessons. On the other hand, when I teach a Sunday morning or small group Bible study, I usually choose to make those transformational lessons.

Either way, first decide if your lesson is going to be primarily informational or transformational. Both lesson formats are valid and have their place in the equipping of the saints. Informational lessons primarily focus on content, whereas transformational lessons primarily focus on life change. Then, after you decide which type of lesson you are going to teach, apply the appropriate teaching principles.

2. Is your goal an InfoTransformational lesson?

Obviously, the next logical question is, "Why not just teach informational lessons that are also transformational?" Well, if you can do this, by all means, do it. However, it is fairly difficult to do for at least three reasons. First, you're limited in the amount of time you have to teach each lesson. Second, teaching a transformational lesson usually takes up all of the teaching time. Last, the teaching principles used to teach a transformational lesson are often different, or even opposite in some cases, from those used to teach an informational lesson.

Throughout the remainder of this lesson, we will focus on one of the foundational teaching principles for how to teach a transformational lesson (which, of course, provides the solution to our riddle). We will also see why this principle makes it difficult to combine an informational lesson with a transformational lesson so that you end up with some sort of InfoTransformational lesson.

Without a doubt, it would be wonderful if you could consistently teach InfoTransformational lessons that present large chunks of information while also transforming lives. Unfortunately, as we shall see, what we often think is an InfoTransformational lesson is, in reality, an informational lesson in disguise. In my experience, most teachers who desire to be transformational, but violate the "teach MORE by teaching LESS" principle, end up teaching informational lessons.

B. For informational lessons, you "Teach More by Teaching More"

When teaching an **informational** lesson, you will use this rather obvious principle: *Teach more by teaching more.*

In other words, when content is the focus of the lesson, then you "teach more" content when you cover more information. You teach more information by covering more verses, background information, and theology. Your listeners may have to write it all down, but at least they have it and can refer to it as needed.

Of course, not all information can be presented at the same rate, but if you present each type of information at an appropriate rate, then the principle for an informational lesson holds true: Teach more by teaching more.

C. For transformational lessons, you "Teach MORE by Teaching LESS"

On the other hand, if you're teaching a **transformational** lesson with the goal of changing a particular area of your listeners' life, then the opposite is true. Instead of "teaching more by teaching more," you have to follow this principle: *Teach MORE by Teaching LESS.*

1. "Teach LESS" in the sense of reducing the breadth of topics or verses covered

In other words, with transformational lessons, you "Teach MORE," in the sense of bringing about more life-change, by "Teaching LESS," in the sense of covering fewer verses, principles, background details, or other interesting, yet semi-related, information.

Even though this principle may initially sound wrong, upon reflection, it makes sense. If you think back over all the lessons or sermons that have significantly changed your life, my guess is each one did not ask you to change five or ten different behaviors, attitudes, or values; rather, they challenged you to change a single element. Granted, that "single change" may have ended up impacting all sorts of different areas in your life, but they all stemmed from the single life-change you made.

If you want to "Teach MORE" in the sense of seeing small, consistent, weekly changes in your listeners' lives, you have to "Teach LESS" by focusing the lesson around a central truth, behavior, issue, choice, action, attitude, value, opinion, prejudice, priority, or commitment. Instead of teaching through large segments of Scripture as you would do in an informational lesson, focus on a smaller segment that deals with a particular area of the listener's life. Then, the bulk of the lesson can concentrate on teaching listeners how to change that one area of their life.

2."Teach ᴸᴱˢˢ" by identifying the lesson's exact goal

One reason teachers cover large segments of Scripture or include various semi-related topics is because they know about the lesson without knowing what the lesson is about. That is, they know the lesson's topic and biblical reference, but they haven't identified the exact point of the lesson or the exact goal they hope to accomplish through the lesson. As a result, without a clear goal, a wide variety of semi-related topics and points all appear to be viable options for inclusion within the lesson.

---

*'Without a clear lesson goal,
a wide variety of semi-related topics and
points all appear to be viable options
for inclusion within the lesson.*

The following scenario is all too common. Jane walks up and asks, "Hey, what's today's lesson about?"

The teacher answers, "It's on Ephesians 2 and 3."

Jane, not really satisfied with that answer, follows up with, "Is there a particular aspect of Ephesians 2 and 3 we are going to look at?"

So the teacher is a little more specific: "We are going to talk about God's grace in our lives."

Still not satisfied, Jane persists, "Oh, that sounds great. What about God's grace?"

Hmm. After thinking through some of the lesson points, the teacher answers with a deeper, more insightful-sounding answer: "We'll be looking at God's rich mercy. And how we·are seated with Jesus … up in the heavenly places. Verse 10 tells us we're his workmanship, created in Christ Jesus for good works. You know what I mean?"

Jane, doing her best to understand, tries to clarify: "So, are we going to look at what it means to be seated with Christ in the heavenly places, about God's rich mercy, what it means to be God's workmanship, how we can know which works God has created for us to do, or … all of that?"

Lesson bloating is the result of knowing about the lesson without knowing what the lesson is about.

Even though Jane was looking for a concise answer, she never found one because there wasn't one. In this case, the lesson really was going to cover everything Jane mentioned along with a few additional topics. If the teacher doesn't identify the core point or principle that needs to be explained, proven, and integrated into listeners' lives, it's all too easy to include diverting ideas, semi-related topics, and random background and cultural information.

Now, don't get me wrong. Background information, word studies, history, and cultural differences are all important for properly understanding the text and should be included within the lesson, but only as this information helps explain and prove the point of the lesson. Too often, information related to the passage displaces information that proves the single unifying point of the passage.

3."Teaching LESS" doesn't mean lessons are shorter; they are just more focused

Of course, the teacher doesn't "Teach LESS" by teaching an abbreviated lesson; instead, the entire lesson focuses on a specific central truth. Likewise, it doesn't mean everyone is learning less; instead, everything they learn relates to this central principle in one way or another.

One part of the lesson explains the biblical text and theology. Another part discusses how to apply the truth. Still, another part deals with common misunderstandings or reasons why listeners may reject the truth. The entire lesson centers around helping listeners accept, believe, apply, and integrate this central truth or principle into their lives.

---

*Too often,
the information related to the passage
displaces the information needed to prove
the single, unifying point of the passage.*

D. Center the lesson around the Sticky Proverb

No doubt, if the entire lesson is going to center around a single central principle or truth, the question arises, "What should that principle or truth be?" And, the answer is, the Sticky Proverb.

Even though we won't fully discuss the Sticky Proverb until the next book in this series, I will introduce it here so you will be familiar with the concept. The Sticky Proverb is a single, brief, memorable nugget of wisdom (or proverb) that you create for each lesson that reveals how the lesson's central truth or principle can be applied in today's culture.

It's "sticky" in the sense that it's easy to remember long after the conclusion of your message, and it's a proverb in the sense that it is a short sentence that reveals how the biblical principle can be applied in our 21st-century lives. It is a short, memorable sentence that reveals how the passage's overarching truth can be used to make daily choices. It is a proverbial rule-of-thumb that helps listeners make life decisions.

It is the main point you want your listeners to learn, remember, and apply. If they get nothing else, the Sticky Proverb is the one point you want them to take home with them because it summarizes the passage's central truth in an applicable way.

1. Listeners forget what they hear

One of the biggest benefits of centering the lesson around the Sticky Proverb is it helps listeners remember the lesson's central truth and application for weeks, months, or even years. It is discouraging when we realize just how quickly listeners forget many of the key life-changing points we make each week.

You have probably even experienced this human weakness yourself. For example, can you recall the main points from last week's sermon, or better yet, from the last lesson you taught? Or what about the lessons you taught last month? Could you list the main points from each of those lessons?

For most, if your lesson includes a series of different topics and principles, by the time you get to the fourth or fifth one, the first three have been forgotten. Even if you make a point that makes listeners realize they need to make changes in their life, it begins to fade in their memory as soon as the next, equally great point is made. Then, that point fades as you move on to the next principle. Often, it is the last thing you say that listeners walk out the door with.

2. Teachers forget what they studied

In fact, we don't just have a hard time recalling last week's lesson, we have a hard time recalling the very lesson we're in the midst of teaching. After all, isn't this why most of us have our notes right in front of us as we teach? So, if we spend all week studying and preparing for our lesson and we still need notes to remind us of what we already decided we are going to say, then is it any wonder why our listeners, who heard each point just one time, forget much of what we say even by the time they get home?

What's the point then? Why teach at all if everyone is going to forget everything we say? Well, first, I didn't say they are going to forget everything. I said they are going to forget much of what we say.

3. Listeners can take notes, but they must be reviewed

Of course, if listeners take notes, it can aid their memory. This is a great practice, especially when the lesson includes large amounts of information. One of the strongest advantages of note taking is this:

Listeners *can* review their notes to remember what you said.

Unfortunately, this advantage has an equally powerful disadvantage:

Listeners *have to* review their notes to remember what you said.

4. Centering your lesson around the Sticky Proverb helps everyone

So, here is what we have so far. Most listeners are going to remember only a few of the things you say. They can take notes, but if they don't review them later, they will still forget. Therefore, by centering your lesson around a single central point (i.e., the lesson's Sticky Proverb), it increases the chances listeners will not only remember this point but apply it as well. Even though you are limiting the number of topics covered in each individual lesson, over the long haul, you will teach MORE by teaching LESS.

III. Sunday school curriculum

As a last example, let's consider curriculum that is often used by Sunday school classes. Sometimes the curriculum includes lessons that cover large sections of Scripture, even up to three or four chapters of the Bible within a single lesson. Understandably, this is done to meet one of the curriculum's primary goals of covering the entire Bible within a certain number of years. However, achieving this goal often results in informational lessons.

Even though every effort is made to create transformational lessons, some of them end up being more informational than transformational. Instead of the lesson centering around a precise, focused Sticky Proverb, it has to center around a more general summary statement that is able to incorporate the entire chunk of Scripture. Similarly, instead of the lesson focusing on a specific area of the listener's life, the lesson has to summarize, condense, and streamline all of the different topics in order to stay within the allotted teaching time.

When teaching this type of lesson, you have a couple of choices. First, you could teach the lesson as it is provided with the understanding that it will have some of the weaknesses discussed earlier. However, a second option would be to focus on a smaller portion of the Scripture. If you choose to do this, prayerfully read through the larger section of Scripture covered within the lesson, find the central passage and truth you believe God wants you to focus on, then use the transformational teaching principles within this series to change the lesson from an informational lesson to a transformational lesson.

As you prepare your lesson, remember, whether you teach six chapters or six verses, you only have a limited amount of time to present your lesson. Ask yourself, "Will I have a greater impact by skimming the surface of a large segment of Scripture or by covering a smaller segment of the passage at a greater depth? Do I believe I will teach more by teaching more or do I believe I will teach MORE by teaching LESS?"

4

How You Teach **MORE**
by Teaching **LESS** *(PART 2)*

Choose the most effective format.
Which one do you use?

Here is the conclusion of the matter:
Fear God and keep his commandments,
for this is the whole duty of man.

— Ecclesiastes 12:13

Chapter Outline / Notes

I. An InfoTransformational lesson format

II. An M28:20 transformational lesson format

III. Which format is more effective?

*W*HAT OFTEN HAPPENS WHEN YOU ASK listeners to make several changes in their life within the same lesson? Simple. They put off deciding how to make all the changes and end up doing nothing. Most people can only focus on one life change at a time, so if you give them a confusing array of changes and choices, it tends to bog them down and hinder them from making any change at all. Instead of giving listeners a handful of principles and letting them choose which ones to apply, it is usually more effective to prayerfully choose the most significant biblical truth and center your lesson around that one truth.

I. An InfoTransformational lesson format

I remember a youth Bible study I once heard on love. In the study, the teacher taught through all thirteen verses in 1 Corinthians 13. His content was somewhat limited in that it dealt with Paul's teaching on love as found in 1 Corinthians 13, but because he tried to cover all thirteen verses, his message had around fourteen points. As a result, he spent only a minute or two on each characteristic of love.

Basically, each point sounded something like this:

Paul tells us "love is patient." The Greek word Paul uses here means "to have patience" or "to be long-suffering." It is responding correctly in the midst of continuous wrongdoing. This means when

your brother or sister irritates you, you should
be patient with them instead of yelling at them.
Or, if your parents do something frustrating, you
need to love them by patiently forgiving them
with a good attitude.

Then, he moved on to the next point, "love is kind,"
and gave a similar explanation, along with one or two
general ways the youth could apply it.

By the end of the lesson, he had skipped through all
thirteen verses presenting most of the obvious truths. He
said a lot, but at the same time, said only a little about any
particular aspect of love. In a sense, he covered everything without covering anything. He told the youth what
they *should be doing*, but didn't deal with the very reasons
why they *weren't doing it*. He told them what they already
knew, without telling them what they needed to know. He
gave vague, generalized exhortations without enumer-
ating any particular steps youth could take to apply the
principles. His goal was an InfoTransformational lesson,
but the lesson contained a lot more information than
transformation.

He was using what I refer to as the Teach-and-Tip lesson format where he taught a little on a verse, gave a quick
tip on how to apply it, then moved on to the next verse
with a little more teaching, another quick application tip,
and on to the next verse. By the end of the lesson, he had
made his way through the text giving various definitions,

explanations, background details, and application tips, but he never made or developed any particular central point.

---

*Covering less material allows time to
articulate the central truth,
substantiate its roots in the text,
illustrate how it can be applied, and
eliminate reasons why it won't be applied.*

He covered a lot of material and gave the youth plenty of things they should change, but as I watched the youth throughout the lesson, I didn't sense many of them were connecting with what was being said. As a matter of fact, it looked like most of them had stopped listening long before the conclusion; they were drawing, whispering, or simply looking out the window.

It would have been more fruitful if the teacher had limited his message to one or two particular aspects of love and then created and presented a more focused outline. By covering less material, the teacher would have had more time to articulate the lesson's central truth or principle, substantiate its roots in the text, illustrate how it can be applied, and eliminate reasons why the youth felt justified in not applying the truth.

II. An M28:20 transformational lesson format

Let's look at another way the teacher could have taught this same lesson. In this second version, the goal is to "Teach MORE by Teaching LESS." That is, the goal is to bring about MORE life-change in regard to one or two particular aspects of love by "teaching LESS" of the content in 1 Corinthians 13. After going through this next version of the lesson, determine which format you believe would have had the greater impact.

An M28:20 Transformational Lesson Format

One of the things I've noticed about life is I'm constantly running into new situations—situations that don't readily reveal the best way to respond or act. Of course, over time, I've gotten better at choosing the best response, but early on, I didn't always make the best choice.

I remember when I was twelve or thirteen, and I had my first boy/girl birthday party. With all these girls everywhere, I was so nervous and excited at the same time, I didn't know how to act. I was just sort of spastic all night.

One of the things I remember doing that night was jumping up on something and giving a thumbs-up every time my parents tried to take a picture. Over and over, picture after picture, I jumped up on a chair, then the table, then a countertop, then halfway up the stairs; each time I gave a thumbs-up. I'm embarrassed just telling you about it, but I was trying to be cool and impress the girls.

My parents kept saying, "Brad, just stand there … Brad, please come down and smile … Brad, why don't you stand beside Karen?" After a while, they gave up and just let me do my own pose. Instead of embarrassing me, they decided to love me by patiently accepting my silly, immature actions.

Did my parents want some normal pictures of my first boy/girl party? Yes. Did they get any? No, they didn't. Did they ask me nicely? Many times. Was I irritating to them? Most definitely. Could they have lost it and embarrassed me in order to coerce me to stop? Yep. In a single sentence, they could have devastated me in front of all my friends (boys and girls) and taken the picture they wanted, but they didn't.

Instead, they were patient with me and loved me because "love is patient." This was a new experience for me, and I was choosing to respond in a wrong way. After asking me to stop a dozen times, they gave up on *what they wanted* so they could love me through that night and help me later.

Now that is love. Sometimes, love is being patient with a brother or sister, father or mother, even when they don't deserve it. Love is patient even when they are driving you crazy and it is going to cost you something you desire. It is patiently doing what is best for them even at your own expense.

Even though you are older now and have learned how to respond to a wide variety of situations, it is easy to forget that your younger brothers or sisters are still figuring these things out for themselves. They, too, want to feel important and accepted by you and your friends, and they don't always go about it the right way, just like you and I didn't go about it the right way the first time we faced a new situation.

Are they irritating when they make kissing sounds while you're talking to your boyfriend or girlfriend on the phone? Absolutely! Are they irritating when they act silly when your friends are over? You bet they are. Could you get them to stop by embarrassing them with a single sentence in front of your friends? No question ... right?

However, Paul tells us, love is patient, patiently doing what is best for your brother or sister even when they are doing what is wrong, driving you crazy, or costing you something (1 Corinthians 13:4). The Greek word used here means "patient" or "long-suffering." Paul says love is long-suffering because most can respond correctly for a day or two, but only genuine love responds correctly day after day, month after month, and yes, even year after year. No doubt, your brother or sister is going to cause you to suffer, and more than likely, it is going to be longer than a day or two.

Even though it is going to take them a few years to grow up, Paul is telling you to love them through this time in their life. He is telling you not to destroy your relationship with them during this phase of life so you can enjoy a healthy friendship with them throughout the remainder of your life, to love them at their worst so you can later enjoy them at their best. He's telling you to love them when they don't deserve it and even when they may use that love to their advantage. This is why Paul says love is long-suffering. It is caring for them even when it costs you. It is a gift given over and over again.

If you'll notice, Jesus tells us the same thing in Matthew 7:12. Loosely translated, he says, "Treat your brother or your sister as you would want an older brother or sister to treat you if you were the one being immature and silly." Loving them may not immediately change their actions, but it will enable God to work through you, and it will define your relationship with them throughout the remainder of your life.

How, then, do we love an irritating person with patience?

Then, throughout the remainder of the study, the teacher would provide a comprehensive biblical answer to the above question. He would fully explain, prove, illustrate, and support the lesson's central truth or principle with the appropriate scriptural text. In addition, because he is dealing with fewer aspects of love (i.e., Teaching LESS), he will have time to deal with common objections the youth may have for why they believe this verse doesn't apply to their specific situation. The following is an example of how these objections can be raised and answered within the study:

> Some of you may be thinking, "Well, you just don't understand my brother or sister. They are so annoying. I think they even annoy me on purpose at times. Even telling my parents doesn't help. I understand I should be patient with them, but when they do this or that, they no longer deserve my patience. Even my friends can't stand to be around them. Actually, I've found that the only way to get them to stop is by embarrassing them."

Now, in all reality, this may be true. Their parents may be doing a poor job of parenting, and their irritating siblings may really be relentless. So, how do they patiently love them in this setting? If you don't deal with the actual struggles your listeners are having, then little will change by telling them simply, "Love is patient; therefore you should be patient." If you don't cut back on the amount of semi-related topics you are presenting and take time to answer the hard, but real-life questions, then your lessons will be informational, not transformational.

III. Which format is more effective?

Now, which of these two Bible studies do you believe would be more effective? The first one covered all thirteen verses in 1 Corinthians 13 telling listeners, "You should do this, and you should do that, and you should do this, and that and this and that." It's a mile wide, but an inch deep.

The second Bible study, on the other hand, first limits the content to verse 4. Then, the remainder of the lesson explains the verse; develops the lesson's central, core truth; demonstrates what this truth would look like in the youth's lives; deals with common objections and rationalizations for why the youth don't believe this verse applies to their specific situation; and challenges the youth to make a specific change in their life.

In my own experience, I have found that the second, more focused Bible study would have the greater impact. Nonetheless, many teachers will still end up delivering the first, more familiar format for a few different reasons. Probably one of the biggest reasons is that this format is far easier to prepare and present. All the teacher needs to do is explain a rather straightforward verse, give a quick application tip, and then move on to the next verse. Second, if they need to make the lesson a little longer, they can just add a few more, "You should do this and that" type verses and they are ready to teach.

> *You can never present what is right*
> *without exposing what is wrong,*
> *and some who do the wrong*
> *would rather fight the right than change.*

On the other hand, an M28:20 transformational lesson format is more difficult and time consuming to develop since you have to figure out the biblical response to real-life questions and issues. Furthermore, when you confront listeners' rationalizations and objections, it isn't always easy since you may experience a fair amount of resistance along the way. You can never present what is right without exposing what is wrong, and some who do the wrong would rather fight the right than change.

We must not allow their resistance, our feelings of inadequacy, or anything else to hinder us from boldly challenging listeners with the Word of God. As we will see in the next chapter, God has clearly called us to feed and grow others through our teaching ministry, so we must learn to overcome obstacles that hinder us from fulfilling that calling.

5

Become One of the Imperfect People God Uses

How to boldly teach and challenge your class despite your past and weaknesses

*Forgetting what is behind and
straining toward what is ahead,
I press on toward the goal
to win the prize for which God has called
me heavenward in Christ Jesus.*

— Philippians 3:13–14

Application

Chapter Outline / Notes

I. **God calls us to pray, prepare, and teach**
   A. Peter made prayer and teaching a top priority

   B. Make time for prayer and preparation

II. **God calls us to care for and feed his sheep**
   A. God called Peter to care for and feed his sheep

   B. God also calls us to care for and feed his sheep

III. **God calls us to Forget It & Press On ... FIPO**
   A. God uses us despite inadequacies

   B. God uses us despite past and future sin

   C. God works through us as he matures us

   D. Our responsibility is to Forget It & Press On

IV. God calls us to fulfill the Great Commission

A. Matthew's last words emphasize the Great Commission

B. Jesus' last words emphasize the Great Commission

C. Teaching is at the center of the Great Commission

D. Jesus calls some teachers to train and equip other teachers

*B*ECOMING A TRANSFORMATIONAL TEACHER IS not only about learning how to transform lives through your teaching; it's also about developing your relationship with God and allowing him to mold you into the person he desires you to become. It's about aligning your view of yourself and your ministry with his views. It's about altering your life to ensure teaching remains a top priority. It's about altering the activities you do or don't get involved in so you can fulfill the Great Commission through your teaching ministry.

The apostle Peter is a great role model for us in this area. Peter started out pretty rough around the edges and didn't even consider himself to be worthy of being in Jesus' presence, but over time, he grew to understand that God wanted to use him to teach others how to live a godly life. As a result, Peter always strove to keep his teaching ministry a priority. Of course, as the church grew, so did the amount of ministry (helping the sick, widows, and orphans; settling disputes; training; teaching; etc.). Even though Peter realized these various ministries were important and needed attention, he was careful to keep prayer and teaching his top priority.

I. God calls us to pray, prepare, and teach
A. Peter made prayer and teaching a top priority
Was there anything wrong with Peter ministering in various areas? Absolutely not! However, God had given Peter the responsibility of teaching, so when the amount of ministry grew to the point of his having to choose one ministry over the other, or when his teaching would suffer

as a result of being involved in another ministry, Peter clearly understood prayer and teaching had to remain his top priority. We see an example of this in Acts 6:1–4.

> In those days when the number of disciples was increasing, the Grecian Jews among them complained against the Hebraic Jews because their widows were being overlooked in the daily distribution of food. So the Twelve gathered all the disciples together and said, "It would not be right for us to neglect the ministry of the Word of God in order to wait on tables. Brothers, choose seven men from among you who are known to be full of the Spirit and wisdom. We will turn this responsibility over to them and will give our attention to prayer and the ministry of the word."

In this passage, Peter is *not* saying, "I'm not going to help because that is not my ministry … you know … I'm a teacher! Not a waiter!" Rather, Peter is saying, "I'm already involved in so much ministry that if I add anything else, the teaching ministry God has given me will suffer."

B. Make time for prayer and preparation

So what's the point? I'm not saying the only ministry you should be involved in is teaching, and I'm not saying you shouldn't take time to relax and enjoy friends, family, and life. Instead, I'm saying your teaching ministry is vital to the church, so if you cannot adequately pray about and prepare for your lesson because of "other activities," then you may need to see if some of these can be reorganized so your teaching ministry remains effective. My prayer is as we grow in our understanding of how God wants to work through us, the priority prayer and teaching have in our lives will grow as well.

II. God calls us to care for and feed his sheep

When thinking about the teacher's role or calling, many view this as a calling to be an educator within the church. That is, their goal is to teach and explain the Bible to their class. However, even though the biblical calling includes explanation, it extends beyond this goal. It is a calling to care for God's children, to feed them from the Word, and to teach them how to live their lives with the Bible as the authority of all that is said.

A. God called Peter to care for and feed his sheep

I realize we often refer to this teaching activity with words such as "school" or "study" as in Sunday school or Bible study, but what you're shooting for is far different than what a teacher shoots for in a school setting. When you teach, the goal extends beyond teaching facts, history, theology, and principles. Instead, it's all about spiritually growing Al, John, Karen, Wayne, Donna, and all the others in your class. Look at what Jesus tells Peter in John 21:14–17.

> This was now the third time Jesus appeared to his disciples after he was raised from the dead. When they had finished eating, Jesus said to Simon Peter, "Simon son of John, do you truly love me more

than these?" "Yes, Lord," he said, "you know that
I love you." Jesus said, "Feed my lambs." Again
Jesus said, "Simon son of John, do you truly love
me?" He answered, "Yes, Lord, you know that I
love you." Jesus said, "Take care of my sheep." The
third time he said to him, "Simon son of John, do
you love me?" Peter was hurt because Jesus asked
him the third time, "Do you love me?" He said,
"Lord, you know all things; you know that I love
you." Jesus said, "Feed my sheep."

Peter had denied knowing Jesus three times, so Jesus
used this threefold calling to ensure Peter knew he was
forgiven and that Jesus still wanted him to feed and take
care of believers. As a result, Peter organized his life and
activities so that he could care for believers and transform their lives through the Word.

B. God also calls us to care for and feed his sheep

Of course, Jesus isn't calling just Peter and pastors to
care for and feed his sheep; he is also calling individuals like you and me. In the same way Peter was forgiven
for denying he even knew Jesus, we also are forgiven for
our sins and commissioned to continue in ministry. And
like Peter's ministry, God doesn't view this as some small,
incidental side ministry in your life; rather, it is a call to
take care of and feed Jesus' sheep. It is far more than reading the text and explaining what occurred; it's changing
lives through the Word. It is a powerful ministry where
God Almighty speaks through his Word, through you,
and into the lives of those within your class.

*Teaching is far more than reading the text
and explaining what occurred;
it's changing lives through the Word.*

III. God calls us to Forget It & Press On ... FIPO
A. God uses us despite inadequacies

However, sometimes we feel more comfortable presenting informational or educational lessons that are "safe"
and ruffle as few feathers as possible. But why? Why don't
we challenge our listeners with the same intensity found
within the biblical text? I think it is because we sometimes
don't believe God would use us to dramatically change
others through "our" teaching. Often, failures, lack of
experience, past events, or past sins have a way of making us feel inadequate or unworthy of being used by God
for anything of significance.

After all, how could God use me if I completely failed
when I tried to do this thing over here, if my education is
somewhat lacking, if I committed these particular sins, or
if that particular sin was committed against me? We need
to rest assured that we all are made from the same cloth
and we all live in the same world. You and I are not alone;
every single person alive has failed many times throughout their life, has a multitude of sins they wish they had
never committed, and has a number of sinful things that
have happened to them that were just plain wrong.

Consider David, son of Jesse. David had seven older
brothers, and in his culture, no one would have expected

David, the youngest, to be chosen as the king of Israel. In our culture, we may not think twice about it, but in the Israelite culture, this was just not done. The firstborn son received a double portion of the inheritance, was the head of the whole family, received a special blessing from his father, and more. Thus, during that time, everyone would have naturally assumed that the eldest, not the youngest, would have been appointed king of Israel.

When God chose David, it became clear that God chose according to his grace and purposes, not according to cultural, community, or family norms or expectations. God did not choose David because of David's cultural or family position; rather, he chose David for his own reasons.

So, if you don't fit the expected mold for a teacher, congratulations, you are among a host of others. God did not call you because you have a picture-perfect past or even because you are currently at the front of the class; rather, he chose you because he wants to work through you by his grace. Your first lesson may not be the best, but most great teachers don't start as great teachers. It takes a commitment on your part, time, training, hard work, and slow growth to develop into a great teacher.

Most great teachers
don't start as great teachers
but develop over time.

B. God uses us despite past and future sin

Notice also how God forgave and used David despite his sin: both past and future. Even though David was a man after God's own heart, God knew full well that David was going to become an adulterous murderer in the near future. Even within our sex-saturated society, David and Bathsheba's sin would be shocking. And yet, even after their sin and repentance, God allowed David to continue to rule, and he allowed both of them to be a part of the lineage of Jesus ("and Jesse the father of King David. David was the father of Solomon, whose mother had been Uriah's wife" [Matthew 1:6]).

You yourself may have committed some secret sins in your past or maybe you feel guilty because of some sin that has been committed against you. You may be wondering how God can use someone like you with a past like that. But he will, even as he did in the lives of many others like David and Bathsheba; Moses, who murdered an Egyptian taskmaster (Exodus 2:11); Tamar, who posed as a prostitute and tricked Judah into impregnating her (Genesis 38:14–19); Peter, who denied he knew Christ at his greatest time of need (John 18:27); and even Paul, who ravaged the church, going from house to house, dragging off men and women and putting them in prison (Acts 8:1).

Granted, we are all different and have different pasts, so no one can understand your exact circumstances, but you are not alone, and you are no less worthy to be used by God than anyone else if you have repented of your sin, forgiven those who have wronged you, and are moving forward with God.

C. God works through us as he matures us

To be perfectly honest, it's a wonder God is able to work through any of us, but he does. God calls and uses people just like you and me to serve him in various ministries throughout the church. It is easy to look at others and assume their life and past are untainted by sin making them more worthy to teach than we are, but this is simply not true. Or maybe we shy away from teaching because we don't believe we are smart enough or have enough formal education, but God uses individuals right where they are, then he grows them into the person he wants them to become.

Look at the apostle Peter. He was a commercial fisherman, and my guess is, Peter did not put an emphasis on his formal education in his earlier years. Plus, when he first met Jesus, he admits his life was full of sin. Look at Peter's own words.

> When Simon Peter saw this, he fell at Jesus' knees and said, "Go away from me, Lord; I am a sinful man!"
>
> —Luke 5:8

Even though Peter's sin, baggage, and limitations were clear for all to see, Jesus called him anyway.

> Then Jesus said to Simon, "Don't be afraid; from now on you will catch men." So they pulled their boats up on shore, left everything and followed him.
>
> —Luke 5:10–11

D. Our responsibility is to Forget It & Press On

The apostle Paul had much to be ashamed of as well. As a young man, he persecuted the church and hurt many believers. Luke shares a little about this in the book of Acts.

> But Saul began to destroy the church. Going from house to house, he dragged off men and women and put them in prison.
>
> —Acts 8:3

Paul had every reason to focus on his past actions and allow them to dictate his future so that they hindered him from being used by God. In order to deal with his own past, he adopted and lived by a principle we should all live by. I refer to it as the Philippians FIPO Principle: Forget It and Press On. It is found in Philippians.

> Brothers, I do not consider myself yet to have taken hold of it. But one thing I do: Forgetting what is behind and straining toward what is ahead, I press on toward the goal to win the prize for which God has called me heavenward in Christ Jesus.
>
> —Philippians 3:13–14

Paul knew that looking back empowers the past to influence the present and enables memories to direct our future. So, he encourages us to forget yesterday's sin so we can focus on Christ within and the good works God has created for us to do. Our past is our past, not our future, so Forget It and Press On.

*Looking back only empowers
the past to change the present and
influence your future.*

After we repent, seek forgiveness, and make any necessary restitution, Paul tells us to let go of the sin, along with the guilt, grief, grudges, bitterness, and anger associated with it. God forgives us and continues to work in us so we can do the good works he has already created for us to do.

> For we are God's workmanship, created in Christ Jesus to do good works, which God prepared in advance for us to do.
> —Ephesians 2:10

So, when we're reminded of how we used to cheat or steal, yet have repented of such acts, Paul tells us to say, "FIPO" (Forget It & Press On) and focus on glorifying God in the future. When we're reminded of how we used to abuse drugs or treat others poorly, we can say, "FIPO," and press on toward the goal to win the prize for which God has called us heavenward in Christ Jesus. When we're reminded of how someone sinned against us, we can "FIPO" it, and strain toward what is ahead.

What all this means is that God has many truths he wants to say through you. He has many lives he wants to change through your teaching. Not through others in your church ... through you. Commit to his calling and FIPO your past.

> As each one has received a special gift, employ it in serving one another as good stewards of the manifold grace of God.
>
> —1 Peter 4:10 NASB

IV. God calls us to fulfill the Great Commission

Often, last words reveal what is most important to an individual. When you drop your child off at a friend's house for a slumber party, what are your last words? Maybe something like this: "Now Jonny, don't forget to say, 'Yes ma'am' and 'yes sir' and to thank them for dinner. Don't run or yell in the house, and don't forget to flush the toilet and put the seat down after you use it. I love you ... have a good time." Those are the most consequential actions you want to make sure Jonny doesn't forget, so you save them till just before he gets out of the car.

A. Matthew's last words emphasize the Great Commission

In his gospel, Matthew also records last words he doesn't want his readers to forget. Of all the truths and principles Jesus taught throughout his ministry, Matthew chose to conclude his gospel with what is often referred to as the Great Commission. Matthew gives us 28 chapters on the life and teaching of Christ but then decides to conclude the entire book with "go and make disciples ... baptizing them ... teaching them to obey everything I have commanded you. And surely I am with you always, to the very end of the age'" (Matthew 28:19–20). Period. That's it. He leaves these words ringing in our ears. You can't miss their importance to Matthew as the final words in his gospel.

B. Jesus' last words emphasize the Great Commission

Why do you think Matthew decided to conclude with the Great Commission? Why did he consider it to be a pivotal command? Well, probably because Jesus had the same view.

Think about it. If you knew your time was short and you were about to see loved ones for the last time, instead of talking about the weather, wouldn't you tell them how much you love them and give final words of encouragement and advice? Of course you would. We all would. We would concentrate on what was most important to us.

Near the end of Jesus' time on earth, he had this type of opportunity with his disciples. He had just a short time to give them a few final instructions. The question is, as Jesus approached the end of his earthly ministry, realizing his time was short, what did he choose to emphasize? The answer: evangelism and teaching.

Let's look again at the Great Commission as found in Matthew 28:18–20:

> Then Jesus came to them and said, "All authority in heaven and on earth has been given to me. There-fore go and make disciples of all nations, baptizing them in the name of the Father and of the Son and of the Holy Spirit, and teaching them to obey

everything I have commanded you. And surely
I am with you always, to the very end of the age."

C. Teaching is at the center of the Great Commission

In light of Jesus' last words, do you believe your teaching ministry is important to him? You had better believe it is! It is central to the Great Commission he has called us to fulfill. Many times, when people think of the Great Commission, they think of evangelism, but that is only the first step. After people are saved, God molds individuals like yourself into M28:20 teachers who will teach them how to grow in their faith and develop into fully committed Christ followers.

*Your teaching ministry
is at the very center of how
your church fulfills the Great Commission.*

D. Jesus calls some teachers to train and equip other teachers

God has called us to go and make disciples. Some fulfill this commission by teaching on a regular basis in a Sunday school class, a small group Bible study, or another similar setting. Others focus on training and equipping leadership using resources like this one that center around training teachers.

Even though we are all familiar with teaching in a small group or Sunday school setting, I would like some of you to be open to the possibility that God may be calling you to a slightly different teaching role, more specifically, to train and equip teachers. For this ministry, you do not need to be the best teacher within your church. Nor do you need to have all the answers. Instead, it means that God has given you a passion to grow and develop your own teaching skills, that he has given you a passion to help others grow and develop their teaching skills, and that you commit to organize ongoing training for the teachers within your church.

Now, whether you train teachers or teach in a small or large group setting, the important thing to remember is if God has called you to teach his Word, he has privileged you with a crucial ministry and responsibility within the church. It's not about having a ministry; it's about changing lives for eternity. It's not about biblical information; it's about Christ-centered transformation.

As you consider how to invest the limited amount of time and energy you possess, notice how much of an impact you can have on others as your teaching changes your listeners' lives, and then, how much their lives impact other people's lives, who then impact others. As we will see in the next chapter, if you wisely invest your time in your teaching ministry, it will ripple from person to person to person.

6

Create a Ripple
That Continues into Eternity

Your impact does not stop at the end of class ... it ripples from person to person to person all the way into eternity

The elders who direct the affairs of the church well are worthy of double honor, especially those whose work is preaching and teaching.

—1 Timothy 5:17

Chapter Outline / Notes

I. **God has given you ... "enough time"**

A. However, is "enough time" ... enough time?

    1. Time doesn't slow for our busy schedules

    2. Early on, it feels as if we have forever

    3. Sooner or later, we all realize "life is short"

    4. Eventually, we all notice our hourglass is emptying

    5. Biblically speaking, life doesn't just seem short; it is short

B. We can't control how quickly life passes but only what happens as it passes

    1. Rather than **let** *life happen, choose* **how** *it happens*

    2. Few activities have the eternal impact teaching has

II. Your teaching impacts multiple generations

A. Listeners come to you weekly for biblical insights

B. You may be a youth's primary source of instruction

C. Your impact extends beyond your listeners' lives

D. Your teaching influences individuals for decades

III. Your teaching matures your church

A. God appoints teachers such as yourself

B. "Eagerly desire the greater gifts"

C. Only teaching is in each of the spiritual gift lists

ECENTLY, DUE TO CONSTRUCTION, our church had to combine several Sunday school classes for nearly a year. This meant that each combined class now had, instead of one or two teachers, more like four, five, or six teachers. Even though the situation was a disruption, it was also a revelation in that it revealed the passion our teachers have for teaching.

For example, during one of the teachers' meetings, the leader stood up and said, "All right, let's break up into our classes and create teaching schedules for the next quarter," and within a minute or two, all the slots were filled. The available slots were scooped up as if they were tickets to win a million dollars.

If you have been asked to be a teacher but have never taught before, you may be asking yourself, "Wow … why is teaching such a priority to them? Why are they so passionate about it? What motivates them to spend hours every week studying and preparing for the lesson?"

Of course, these are great questions that have equally great answers, as we will see shortly. In this chapter, we will look at the priority God places on you as a teacher, how he works through you to mature those within your church, how your lessons can still be impacting lives a hundred years from now, how you can transform lives as well as educate minds, and last, how you fulfill the Great Commission (Matthew 28:19–20) when you teach.

I. God has given you ... "enough time"

A. However, is "enough time" ... enough time?

We all want our lives to count for God's eternal kingdom. We want to be part of something bigger than ourselves, something that will have a significant eternal impact on our families and others. However, accomplishing this within our limited time constraints is challenging.

1. Time doesn't slow for our busy schedules

How many times have you woken up Monday morning and asked yourself, "Boy, how did we get all the way back to Monday again? Where in the world did last week go?" If we're not careful, a week can slip by before we achieve most of what we wanted to achieve. An entire summer can slip by in what felt like three or four weeks. Then, after what feels like another month or two, it's Christmas and we're handing out presents. Another few months and it's summer again. What felt like four or five months is a year, and what felt like a year is two years.

2. Early on, it feels as if we have forever

When we're young, it feels as if we have forever to fulfill our hopes and dreams, but before we know it, we've graduated from school and a significant portion of our life has come and gone. At that point, we may no longer feel as if we have forever, but it still seems as if we have a really long time. Unfortunately, these feelings deceive many into squandering much of their lives. We have all heard the quote "time is money," but really, "time is life." If we waste our time, we waste our life.

Time is Life…
wasted time is a wasted life.

3. Sooner or later, we all realize "life is short"

Do you realize that by the time you are 35 to 40 years old, half of your life has come and gone and more than half of your healthiest years are now a past event? That's difficult for most of us to accept. Once we let it sink in a little, we can better relate to the perspective Job and James had on life.

> My days are swifter than a weaver's shuttle, and they come to an end without hope. Remember, O God, that my life is but a breath.
>
> —Job 7:6–7

> What is your life? You are a mist that appears for a little while and then vanishes.
>
> —James 4:14

4. Eventually, we all notice our hourglass is emptying

If an hourglass measured the years of our life, then, when we are young, the top half of the hourglass would be full of sand. Because it looks as if we have enough sand to live forever, we dream of everything we want to do throughout our lifetime.

As we set out to fulfill these dreams, our hourglass gets lost among all the activities we are pursuing. Most of us never even notice the sand trickling away until much later in life. For me, this moment didn't come until after I was married and had kids in grade school. As they dreamed of everything they wanted to do throughout their lifetime, it reminded me of how I, too, used to dream when I was … their age … and poof, out of nowhere, my hourglass reappeared right in front of me.

As I looked at it for the second time, I wondered how in the world almost half my sand had already passed through that little hole. Even as I sat there studying the change in the sand levels, the sand continued to trickle down from the "what-I-have-left" top portion of the hourglass to the "what-is-now-a-past-event" bottom portion. Every moment I live drains the sand that remains. I cannot save it, store it, or ration it.

King David says it this way:

As for man, his days are like grass, he flourishes like a flower of the field; the wind blows over it and it is gone, and its place remembers it no more.
— Psalm 103:15–16

You have made my days a mere handbreadth; the span of my years is as nothing before you. Each man's life is but a breath.
— Psalm 39:5

———

Time … you can't
save it, store it, or ration it.
You can't control how quickly it passes,
only what happens as it passes.

———

5. Biblically speaking, life doesn't just seem short; it is short

The Bible warns us of the brevity of life. It tells us that we have barely a scoop of sand in our hourglass to accomplish everything we want to accomplish. We have just enough time to do a couple of things, bloom for a short season, then the wind will blow, and as King David said, "its place remembers it no more."

Psalm 90:10 says it all:

> The length of our days is seventy years—or eighty, if we have the strength; yet their span is but trouble and sorrow, for they quickly pass, and we fly away.

B. We can't control how quickly life passes but only what happens as it passes

So, what if the time God gives us isn't enough to achieve all of our dreams and goals (Psalms 39:4; 139:16; Job 14:5; 21:21)? We're all losing sand at a rate of 60 grains per minute. You don't know how many grains you have left, but what you have is yours to use as you choose. You can't control how quickly it passes but only what you do as it passes. We all begin with some sand and end with none; what happens between those two points is your decision. Take a look at the sand levels in your own hourglass and consider these questions:

- First, if you live an average life span of seventy to eighty years, how much sand do you have left? Of course, no one is guaranteed seventy to eighty years worth of sand, so you really don't know how much is in the top, what-you-have-left portion of your hourglass. Still, assuming you have, say, eighty years', how many productive years do you have left?

- Second, have you significantly impacted eternity with the sand that has already passed?
- Third, as the sand that remains trickles away, are you currently impacting others for Christ? Are you involved in others' lives right now?
- Last, are the goals, dreams, interests, and activities you are currently pursuing worthy of the sand you are exchanging for them? When tomorrow comes and the exchange is complete, what will you have in its place?

*1. Rather than **let** life happen, choose **how** it happens*

No matter how much sand has passed or how much remains, life is but a breath. "You are a mist that appears for a little while and then vanishes" (James 4:14). You may be in full bloom right now, but soon, the wind is going to blow your direction and your life will be a past event (Psalm 103:15–16). The only thing you can say with confidence is "if it is the Lord's will, we will live and do this or that" (James 4:15).

What you choose to do with your days and evenings is important because you are exchanging a portion of your sand for each activity. You may only pay a few dollars a month for cable TV, but its true cost is the night's worth of sand you give in exchange for it. Personal goals we pursue are also costly. Are the benefits they bring worth the exchange? Are these activities thieves who slip into the night with your most precious resource?

Now, we all need time to relax, rest, have fun, and enjoy our friends, family, and life itself. We just need to make sure our lives are balanced and biblical. We need to make sure we aren't just LETTING life happen by consciously CHOOSING how it happens. Decide where you want to go and consistently move in that direction.

2. Few activities have the eternal impact teaching has

We all are involved in various ministries according to the spiritual gift(s) God has given us, but in this book, we have focused on how God uses those with the gift of teaching to impact eternity as a Bible teacher. God does not need superstars; rather, he desires willing servants. He does not need those who have monuments dedicated to them; rather, he seeks those who will dedicate themselves to study, prayer, and teaching others how to live a godly life. If you desire to impact others, few activities offer the eternal opportunities teaching offers.

II. Your teaching impacts multiple generations
A. Listeners come to you weekly for biblical insights

When you think about all the different ministries within the church, teaching has one of the biggest impacts on others. Think about it: every week, those within your class give you 30 to 60 minutes to teach them how to live their lives. That's remarkable! Where else in the world would an individual, much less an entire group of people, give you this opportunity? It's really quite amazing. Your class may include doctors, lawyers, engineers, schoolteachers, moms, dads, grandparents ... anyone and everyone. They come to you weekly for how to live a godly life!

B. You may be a youth's primary source of instruction

If you teach children, youth, or college students, you may provide more life instruction in a year's time than some of them will receive from their family throughout their entire lifetime. Let me say that again: if you teach children, youth, or college students, you may provide more life instruction in a year's time than some of them will receive from their family throughout their entire lifetime. Your ministry within their lives has an immense influence. You may feel as if nothing is sinking in, but it is. As a teacher, God gives you a wonderful opportunity and a priceless privilege to impact students' lives in ways few others can or ever will.

C. Your impact extends beyond your listeners' lives

Plus, your teaching impacts not only your listeners' lives but also everyone connected to them, including their spouse, children, extended family, neighbors, coworkers, those within your church, and many others.

To illustrate, let's say a couple in your class is headed toward divorce, but instead of continuing down that path, they decide to work out their differences because of your weekly teaching. Their decision impacts not only their own life but also the lives of many others.

For example, the couple will remain together and bypass the pain and suffering involved in divorce. The couple's children will likewise be saved from the pain, rejection, and other ill effects of divorce. Those ill effects often influence how the children treat others, including their own spouse and children. So, your teaching may even have a part in preventing their children from getting a divorce and starting the cycle all over again. Even the couple's parents, now nearing the end of their lives, won't have to painfully watch their child's family fall apart.

What may appear to be simple, straightforward Bible lessons, week after week, may in reality be life-changing studies that slowly mold your listeners' lives as well as the lives of the next two or three generations that follow them. This is why teaching is such an honor and a privilege.

D. Your teaching influences individuals for decades

I say all this to remind you of your importance as a teacher and to keep you from viewing each lesson as just one more lesson you have to prepare and teach. I say this to remind you that next week's lesson may, in fact, impact people's lives 100 years from now. It is a reminder that each time you teach, you are throwing a nugget of truth into the pond of your listeners' lives. The resulting ripples can extend in all directions for 5, 10, 50, 100, or more years as your teaching impacts your listeners' lives, and as their lives impact their children's lives, which impact their children's lives, and so forth.

III. Your teaching matures your church
A. God appoints teachers such as yourself

As you can see, it is no wonder why God places such an importance on teachers. In 1 Corinthians 12, Paul corrects the Corinthians for overemphasizing some of the spiritual gifts. Then, in verse 28, after discussing the various gifts and offices within the church, Paul numerically highlights three of the gifts that should be emphasized and desired because of their ability to impact the entire body of Christ.

Look at what Paul says:

> And in the church God has appointed first of all apostles, second prophets, third teachers, then workers of miracles, also those having gifts of healing, those able to help others, those with gifts of administration, and those speaking in different kinds of tongues.
>
> —1 Corinthians 12:28

B. "Eagerly desire the greater gifts"

Teaching is right there at the top of the list. Paul emphasizes we should desire the greater gifts since they have a greater impact on and are a greater benefit to the entire body of Christ.

> Are all apostles? Are all prophets? Are all teachers? Do all work miracles? Do all have gifts of healing? Do all speak in tongues? Do all interpret? But eagerly desire the greater gifts.
>
> —1 Corinthians 12:29–31

When Paul says, "eagerly desire the greater gifts," he is referring to the gifts that help the entire body of Christ, including proclaiming the gospel and teaching God's Word. But why? Why should we eagerly desire these greater gifts? It is because of how they, first, bring people into the body of Christ, and second, how they bring unity, mutual edification, and growth.

C. Only teaching is in each of the spiritual gift lists

This emphasis on the gift and ministry of teaching is found elsewhere in Scripture, even in indirect ways. For example, if you look at the different places where spiritual gifts are listed in the Bible, you will find that no one passage gives an exhaustive list of all the gifts.

Romans 12:6-8	1 Corinthians 12:8-10, 28	Ephesians 4:11	1 Peter 4:10-11
• Prophecy	• Administration	• Apostles	• *Speaks*
• Service	• Apostle	• Prophets	• Serves
• *Teaching*	• Faith	• Evangelists	
• Exhortation	• Healing	• Pastors and	
• Giving	• Helps	*Teachers*	
• Leadership	• Miracles		
• Mercy	• Prophecy		
	• *Teaching*		
	• Tongues		
	• Word of Wisdom		
	• Word of Knowledge		
	• Interpretation of Tongues		
	• Distinguishing between spirits		

What is interesting, though, is the only gift listed in all four of these texts is teaching. Obviously, the authors weren't given a memo telling them to always include the gift of teaching; instead, each time the gifts were listed, teaching was always included because of its importance to the church.

————

Your teaching ministry is God's gift to you; committing to it is your gift to God.

————

We have only brushed the surface of what the Bible has to say about the importance of teachers within the church. I hope you realize how your teaching ministry is more than worthy of the time you invest in it. Your teaching ministry is at the very center of how your church fulfills the Great Commission as given in Matthew 28:19–20. Every church committed to fulfilling the Great Commission must have teachers who are committed to becoming M28:20 teachers who teach listeners to obey. The sand that remains in your hourglass is yours to use as you choose. Carefully consider what you can gain in exchange for that which remains.

In the next book in this series, *Teaching to TRANSFORM Not Inform 2: How to Teach a Transformational Sunday School Lesson...STEP-BY-STEP*, you will learn a simple, practical, step-by-step process for developing and teaching Bible lessons that have transformation as their primary teaching goal.

It will show you how to grab and hold your listeners' attention throughout the lesson, how to create a Visual Anchor that will enable them to remember your lesson for years, how to create a Sticky Proverb so they know how to apply the lesson, how to help listeners around Roadblocks that hinder them from obeying the truth, how to give a challenge listeners can commit to, along with many other transformational teaching principles.

To obtain more information and find out how you can get started with the next book/seminar in the *Teaching to Transform Not Inform* series, visit our website at www.M2820.com.

Appendix: Quotations

*Information and Explanation
are foundational to our teaching, but
transformation is the goal.*

. . . .

*Even though listeners may comprehend
your lesson, roadblocks hinder them
from personally accepting it.*

. . . .

*Listeners believe
some principles are universally true,
but not personally applicable.*

. . . .

*Unaddressed pink elephants
can't help but block the path that
leads from the head to the heart.*

. . . .

*Without a clear lesson goal,
a wide variety of semi-related topics and
points all appear to be viable options
for inclusion within the lesson.*

. . . .

*Lesson bloating is the result of
knowing about the lesson without
knowing what the lesson is about.*

. . . .

Too often,
the information related to the passage
displaces the information needed to prove
the single, unifying point of the passage.

. . . .

Covering less material allows time to
articulate the central truth,
substantiate its roots in the text,
illustrate how it can be applied, and
eliminate reasons why it won't be applied.

. . . .

You can never present what is right
without exposing what is wrong,
and some who do the wrong
would rather fight the right than change.

. . . .

Teaching is far more than reading the text
and explaining what occurred;
it's changing lives through the Word.

. . . .

Most great teachers
don't start as great teachers
but develop over time.

. . . .

Looking back only empowers
the past to change the present and
influence your future.

. . . .

Your teaching ministry
is at the very center of how
your church fulfills the Great Commission.

. . . .

Time is Life . . .
wasted time is a wasted life.

. . . .

Time . . . you can't
save it, store it, or ration it.
You can't control how quickly it passes,
only what happens as it passes.

. . . .

Your teaching ministry is God's gift to you;
committing to it is your gift to God.

. . . .

Develop Transformational Teachers

Teaching to Transform Not Inform 1:
Foundational Principles for Making
an Informational Sunday School Lesson…
TRANSFORMATIONAL

People visit Bible studies they are invited to, but they join the ones that center around life-altering teaching. They join classes whose teachers are committed to making disciples, not by "teaching them the Bible," but by "teaching them to obey the Bible" (Matthew 28:20).

The series, *Teaching to **Transform** Not Inform*, equips teachers to change informationally or educationally oriented lessons into life-altering transformational lessons. It reveals how to teach not only the head but also the heart, which results in changed lives.

Satisfaction Guaranteed: We give a full, hassle-free, money-back guarantee for all our products. If you aren't completely satisfied, by all means, please return the item within 60 days for a prompt, courteous, and full refund. Absolutely no risks for you! Call now and get started.

Additional Resources:
• **DVD Video Companion for Teaching To Transform Not Inform Vol.1:** In this companion DVD, Dr. Simon leads your teachers through this series helping them become transformational teachers.

• **Extra Books** (ISBN: 978-1-939257-11-6)

Get Started Today …
To order books & DVDs for a group, see www.M2820.com for bulk pricing.

Grow Your Sunday School Classes

Teaching to TRANSFORM Not Inform 2:
How to Teach a Transformational
Sunday School Lesson...
STEP-BY-STEP

In Matthew 28:19–20, Jesus gives teachers a clear and concise teaching goal: *"Therefore go and make disciples... teaching them to obey everything I have commanded you."* He did not say, teach people *what* to obey or even *how* to obey; rather, Jesus said, *"make disciples... teaching them TO OBEY."* As a result, he made life-altering transformation (not simply information or education) our primary teaching goal.

If you desire to fulfill the Great Commission through your teaching ministry, this book will place at your fingertips a simple, practical, step-by-step process for how you can teach life-altering lessons that use information and explanation to bring about transformation in your listeners' lives.

Additional Resources:
• **DVD Video Companion for Teaching to TRANSFORM Not Inform Vol.2:** In this companion DVD, Dr. Simon leads your teachers through this series helping them become transformational teachers.

• **Extra Books** (ISBN: 978-1-939257-21-5)

Get Started Today ...
To order books & DVDs for a group, see www.M2820.com for bulk pricing.

Host a Live Training Event

If you are interested in hosting a live *Teaching to TRANSFORM Not Inform* training seminar for teachers in your church and/or area, visit www.M2820.com and request additional information.

Each seminar can be tailored to fit the specific needs of your church or group.